Text:
Ingrid van den Berg

Photography:
Heinrich van den Berg
Philip & Ingrid van den Berg

HPH Publishing

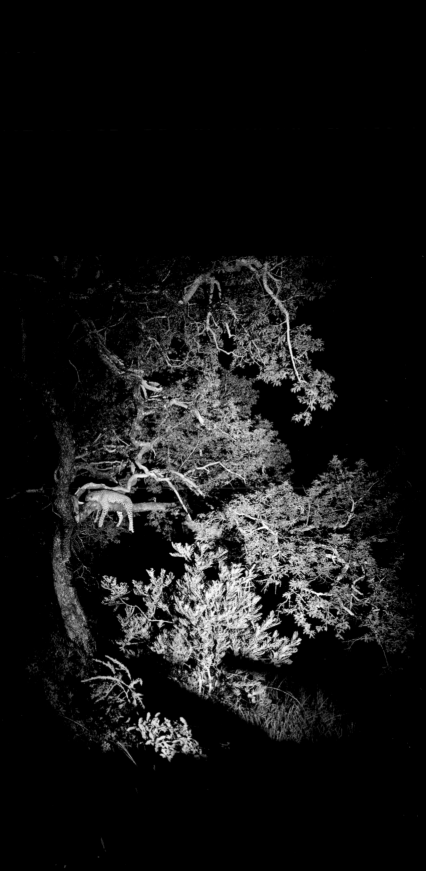

Contents

Get the most from your game drive 6
Eastern bushveld 16
How to use this book 18
The Big 5 20
Killers and scavengers 22
Small carnivores 36
The giants 56
Antelopes 70
Other mammals 104
Reptiles 122
Birds 126
Tracks 180

Get the most from your game drive

The best time of day

Start your drive as early in the morning as possible, and continue until approximately 10am. Resume in mid-afternoon and stay out until sunset, or later if you have a guide with you.

The early morning and late afternoon trigger all kinds of activities in the African bush. This is when many animals are most active; the transition from dark to light finds nocturnal animals scurrying to their daytime hiding places, leopards doing their last rounds, hyena cubs playing outside their den, and lions finishing off their night-time kill. Diurnal animals leave their sleeping places, sun and groom themselves or each other, and start foraging. At dusk, diurnal animals go to rest and the nocturnal ones appear.

Drives during the middle of the day can be disappointing. Many animals are resting in the shade of trees, ruminants are chewing the cud and predators are often are often found sleeping or lying flat and therefore not easily seen.

Some animals, however, remain active during the entire day. Bulk herbivores such as elephants continue grazing or browsing, and baboons and monkeys forage all day, often in trees or simply sit in groups socialising and interacting with one another. Predators that are sometimes active during the heat of the day are cheetahs, wild dogs and some of the mongooses.

Look and listen

Drive slowly, be alert and always expect the unexpected. Look deep into the bush, have patience and watch for movement; the flick of an ear or whisk of a tail. Camouflage is vital for survival in the bush and colours and shapes blend perfectly into their surroundings. Listen for telltale sounds and alarm calls of animals and birds. The 'alert' posture of antelope is another sure sign that they suspect danger.

Where to look

Notice different habitats and know what to expect in which places. Some animals have a specific habitat preference. Lions can be expected in almost all habitats while leopards will never go far from cover. Primates depend on trees for food and safety, and hippos need water deep enough to submerge their bodies. Klipspringers live on rocky outcrops, but grazers are found in herds in the open where they feed on different types and heights of grasses. Browsers tend to be solitary or in small groups. They feed at different heights and from different types of plants.

How to drive

Approach animals slowly and in an indirect way. Give them enough space so as not to feel threatened. Shy animals (especially birds) should be approached in stages. If you get too close, they will feel threatened and flee. Animals will not attack unless provoked to do so. Give approaching elephants enough space to pass, and switch off your engine and anything else making a noise. Animals do not usually associate humans with vehicles. Stay in your vehicle at all times. Do not break the outline of the vehicle with any part of your body by standing up, waving or leaning out of a window.

Binoculars

Binoculars are not essential, but will enhance your enjoyment during game drives. A good pair of binoculars will focus sharply both on near and distant objects, show only one image when viewing, and have coated lenses to reduce the amount of light loss as it passes through the optical system.

Binoculars have two specifying numbers, e.g. 7 x 50. The first number indicates the power of magnification and the second depicts the diameter in millimetres of the objective lens (the big end of the binoculars). The most suitable binoculars are those with a magnification power of

between seven and 10. The higher the power, the greater the magnification, but the steadier your hands should be. The larger the objective lens, the more light it transmits, increasing brightness of the image, but the field of view becomes smaller and the binoculars heavier. Favourite game viewing binoculars are 7 x 35, 8 x 32, and 10 x 42.

Photography

Take memories back home. Digital cameras are easy to use. Make sure you get a sharp photograph by setting the ISO to about 400. To avoid camera shake, try to keep the shutter speed faster than the length of the lens, i.e. if you are using a 100mm lens, set the ISO and f-stop so that the shutter speed is 1/125 per second or faster.

It is not always possible to get close to animals, and telephoto lenses are therefore very useful. The most practical lens is anything between 100mm and 400mm. The best light is just after sunrise and just before sunset. Try to keep the sun behind you to eliminate shadows on the animal. When the light is bad, use a flash. If the flash is not strong enough to light the animal, increase your ISO setting to about 800 ISO.

The most important rule in photography is: Look first; then photograph.

Eastern bushveld

Bushveld is the colloquial term for savannah, which in turn can be described as wooded grassland. Its essential features are deciduous trees with an understorey of grass. There are more than 40 different kinds of savannah, depending on rainfall, vegetation and other factors. Most game reserves in southern Africa are found in the bushveld regions of the subcontinent. This Safari Guide applies to the eastern bushveld game reserves and parks in southern Africa.

These reserves rank among the best destinations for premier wildlife viewing in Africa. They include reserves in the Eastern Cape, KwaZulu-Natal (including Zululand and Maputaland), Swaziland, the Kruger National Park, private reserves in the Greater Kruger, and the Limpopo Transfrontier Park, which straddles conservation areas across South Africa, Mozambique and Zimbabwe. The guide is also applicable to reserves in the Limpopo Province and most areas in Botswana.

The bushveld is home to over 200 larger mammals, more than 500 bird species and a wealth of reptiles, amphibians, fish and invertebrates. This Safari Guide includes a selection of mammals, birds and a reptile that can be encountered on game drives in the eastern part of the country. Typical semi-arid bushveld species such as springbok, gemsbok, red hartebeest, brown hyena, suricate, bateared and silver foxes are not included.

How to use this book

Common name
(Scientific name)

tick box

Afrikaans name (A)   German name (G)
French name (F)   Zulu name (Z)

This section gives an indication of the kind of habitat where the animal can be expected and is likely to be found.

It also highlights one or more interesting facts about it. Animals encountered on game drives can be from the entire spectrum of the animal world, but this booklet concentrates on the larger mammal species, a few small species and the birds that may be seen.

This last section gives even more information, but in a condensed way. Symbols and abbreviations are used and information is in point form.

♀ = female   ♂ = male
☼ = diurnal   ☾ = nocturnal
☼ ☾ = both diurnal and nocturnal
☼(☾) = predominantly diurnal
(☼)☾ = predominantly nocturnal

Please note:
The values for shoulder height, length, mass, gestation and life expectancy can vary and are meant to give an approximate indication for purposes of comparison.

Indicates chapter heading

Sighting rating

★   You will see this animal around every corner.

★ ★   Don't stop too long – you will see it again.

★ ★ ★   Stop and have a cup of tea while you watch it.

★ ★ ★ ★   Put down your tea – this is a special sighting.

★ ★ ★ ★ ★   Slam on the brakes and spill your tea.

★ ★ ★ ★ ★

The Big 5

For centuries man has coexisted and competed with wild animals. In Africa, a few of the most formidable and fiercest have entrenched their place in the psyche of man: the lion with its awe-inspiring power and hunting skills; the mysterious and elusive leopard with its stunning coat; the unpredictable buffalo with its ebony flanks and horns of steel; the temperamental rhino with its insatiable appetite; and the charismatic elephant, the largest animal on land.

Although these five species are not the only ones that are rare, interesting, large, powerful or dangerous, they have captured man's imagination and trophy hunters and nature lovers refer to them as the Big Five. Since they require spacious surrounds, they are mainly confined to large national parks and game reserves.

To encounter any of the Big Five on a game drive is the aspiration of many, but to find all of them on a single game drive is a rare privilege. The African bush is, however, more varied than just the famous Big Five. Enjoy the marvels and mysteries of all the creatures from the tiniest to the most ferocious. Notice the insects, flowers and trees; look out for interactions within species and inter-relationships between different living things; note the vegetation patterns and the nature of the soils; breathe the fresh air; and enjoy being in Africa.

Leopard

African Buffalo

Lion

White Rhinoceros

African Savannah Elephant

★ ★ ★

Black-backed Jackal
(Canis mesomelas)

Rooijakkals/Swartrugjakkals (A)   Schabrackenschakal (G)

Chacal à chabraque (F)   iMpungushe (Z)

The black-backed jackal is widely distributed and not very popular with farmers because it may kill small livestock such as sheep and goats. Its characteristic saddle of black and silver hair distinguishes it from the side-striped jackal, which is particularly shy and seldom seen.

A jackal pair forms a partner bond for life and an individual will find another mate only if one partner dies. Both sexes mark and defend a territory and help to raise the young. The mated pair often forages together or shares food when foraging singly.

Active: (☼) ☾

Shoulder height: 38cm

Mass: ♂ 8kg ♀ 7.4kg

Social structure: only one partner, pair bond and territorial

Collective noun: a skulk of jackals

Gestation: 60–65 days (two months)

Life expectancy: approximately 10 years

Enemies: lion, leopard and large birds of prey

Killers and scavengers

★ ★ ★ ★

Side-striped Jackal
(Canis mesomelas)

Witkwasjakkals (A)   Streifenschakal (G)
Chacal à flancs rayés (F)   iMpungushe (Z)

Although side-striped jackals have a much wider dis-
tribution than black-backed jackals in Africa, they are
not common in the southern African sub-region. They
prefer wetter, wooded areas and avoid open country.

This jackal appears overall grey from a distance, but
many have a distinctive off-white lateral band and a
broad white tip to the tail. It is slightly larger than the
black-backed jackal. The side-striped jackal is omnivo-
rous and eats a variety of plants as well as warm-blood-
ed animals, reptiles, insects and carrion.

Active: (☼) ☾
Shoulder height: 40cm–48cm
Mass: ♂ 9kg ♀ 8kg
Social structure: single, pairs, small family groups
Collective noun: a skulk of jackals
Gestation: 57–60 days (two months)
Life expectancy: approximately 10 years
Enemies: lion, leopard and large birds of prey

24

Killers and scavengers

★★★★★

African Wild Dog
(Lycaon pictus)

Wildehond (A)   Afrikanischer Wildhund (G)
Cynhyène (F)   iNkontshana/iNkentshana (Z)

Wild dogs can be encountered unexpectedly, anywhere, at any time. It is the most specialised of all dogs, hunts in packs and preys on medium-sized antelope. When they make a kill, they will swallow whole pieces of meat, which on their return to their den will be regurgitated for the pups and injured individuals that stayed behind.

Only the alpha pair in the pack reproduces and leads the pack. The males of the pack are related and stay in their birth-pack, while females move out when the pack gets too big. Each member has a rank order and helps to raise the young.

Active: ☀
Shoulder height: 75cm
Mass: ♂ 25kg ♀ 20kg
♂ + ♀ similar in appearance
Social structure: large social packs with a breeding pair
Collective noun: a pack of wild dogs
Gestation: approximately 2.5 months (10 weeks)
Life expectancy: approximately 10 years
Enemies: man

Killers and scavengers

★★★★

Spotted Hyena
(Crocuta crocuta)

Gevlekte hiëna (A) Fleckenhyäne (G)
Hyène tachetée (F) iMpisi (Z)

This sturdily built, large, formidable scavenger and predator is often encountered early in the morning, walking along the road returning to its den. The clan is a matriarchal society with the dominant and other females being larger than the males. It is untrue that these animals are bisexual, but a flap of skin that resembles the male organ covers the reproductive tract of the female.

Hyenas serve a vital purpose in the ecology of an area because they help to clear the bush of decomposing carcasses, and prey on dying or infirm animals. This helps to maintain healthy animal populations.

Active: (☼) ☾
Shoulder height: ♂ 79.4cm ♀ 80.2cm
Mass: ♂ 62.5kg ♀ 68.2kg
♂ smaller than ♀
Social structure: matriarchal clan system with rank order
Collective noun: a clan or cackle of hyenas
Gestation: 110 days (four months)
Life expectancy: approximately 20–25 years
Enemies: lion but also leopard and wild dog

Killers and scavengers

★ ★ ★ ★ ★

Lion

(Panthera leo)

Leeu (A)   Löwe (G)

Lion d'Afrique (F)   iBubesi (Z)

Lions have no specific habitat preference and can be encountered anywhere, except in forests. In the early morning they sometimes rest on the road or are found on a kill. Different prides have different hunting preferences and patterns. The commonest prey is impala, zebra and wildebeest, but some prides regularly kill buffalo, giraffe, and in Savuti, even elephant.

In a lion pride, all the females will be related and the cubs and sub-adults will have been fathered by the male coalition in control of the pride. When a new male coalition takes over a pride, they usually kill all the cubs of the previous males, so that the females can come on heat sooner to bear the new coalition's own offspring.

Active: (☀) ☾

Shoulder height: 1.2m

Mass: ♂ 190kg–200kg ♀ 126kg

♂ with mane appearing in third year

Social structure: pride related ♀'s and brotherhood ♂'s, social

Collective noun: a pride, sault, troop, or sowse of lions

Gestation: 105 days (3.5 months)

Life expectancy: approximately 20 years

Killers and scavengers

Female

★★★★★

Leopard
(Panthera pardus)

Luiperd (A)   Leopard (G)
Panthère/Léopard (F)   iNgwe (Z)

Although well represented in places, its shy secretive ways and mainly nocturnal habits are reasons for it being rarely sighted. This is the most widespread of all predators since it has the broadest habital tolerance of all. Beautiful, powerful and stealthy, it surely is the prize encounter on all game drives.

The leopard's method of hunting is stalking and then pouncing on to the prey, taking it by surprise. The large head and neck are essential for holding and subduing the kill, which is often hoisted up a tree to get it out of reach of other predators.

Active: (☼) ☾
Shoulder height: ♂ 77cm ♀ 66cm
Mass: ♂ 63kg ♀ 37kg
♂ bigger and heavier than ♀
Social structure: solitary, territorial
Collective noun: a leap, leep or lepe of leopards
Gestation: 106 days (3.4 months)
Life expectancy: approximately 20 years
Enemies: lion, wild dog, hyena

Killers and scavengers

★★★★★
Cheetah
(Acinonyx jubatus)

Jagluiperd (A)

Guépard (F)

Gepard (G)

iNgulule (Z)

The cheetah needs bushes, grass or other cover to get within sprinting range of its prey. It is built for speed: light-boned, long thin-legged, short necked, with a slender body and a long tail. It can attain a speed of up to 100km per hour, making it the fastest mammal on land.

The unsheathed claws are less retractile than those of other cats, so that the claws stay out to give the cheetah grip when chasing prey. Their bird-like chirp or whistling call is unlike that of any of the other cats.

Active:

Shoulder height: ♂ 90cm ♀ 75cm

Mass: ♂ 65kg ♀ 35kg

♂ + ♀ similar in appearance

Social structure: breeding ♂ territorial, often has a coalition partner

Collective noun: a coalition of cheetahs

Gestation: 90–98 days (three months)

Life expectancy: approximately 15 years

Enemies: lion, leopard and hyena will kill its young and chase it off its prey

Killers and scavengers

Caracal/Desert Lynx
(Caracal caracal)

Rooikat (A)   Wüstenluchs (G)
Caracal (F)   iNdabushe (Z)

A sighting of caracal in the wild is always a special one. Being shy, well camouflaged and nocturnal, it is rarely seen, although it is plentiful. It inhabits plains, mountains and rocky hills, and seems to need woody vegetation for cover. A good climber and jumper, it is an awesome predator, sometimes killing prey much larger than itself.

   This is the heaviest of the small cats and is the African version of the lynx. The tufts at the ends of the ears are distinctive and probably serve to accentuate the ears in interaction with other individuals. In farming areas, it is regarded as a problem animal.

Active: (☼) ☾
Shoulder height: ♂ 48cm ♀ 43cm
Mass: ♂ 13kg ♀ 10kg
Social structure: solitary and territorial
Collective noun: a pair of caracals
Gestation: 62–81 days (between two and three months)
Life expectancy: approximately 12 years
Enemies: man, leopard and eagles

Aardwolf
(Proteles cristatus)

Aardwolf/Maanhaarjakkals/Erdwolf (A) Erdwolf (G)

Protèle (F) iNgci (Z)

The aardwolf is widespread but seldom seen because of its nocturnal habits. This slender animal looks like a miniature striped hyena but it eats insects, particularly grass-eating termites on overgrazed areas. It gathers the termites with its broad sticky tongue.

Owing to their specialised diet, they have small weak teeth and are therefore not capable of dealing with larger prey. Some stock farmers ignorantly believe they are a threat to livestock and are therefore relentlessly perse-cuted. Although they mostly hide in abandoned aardvark holes, they are able to excavate their own burrows, where they rest during the day.

Active: (☼) ☾
Shoulder height: 50cm
Mass: ♂ 9kg ♀ 8.7kg
Social structure: only one partner, territorial,
pairs within territories
Collective noun: a pair of aardwolves
Gestation: 90–100 days (three months)
Life expectancy: approximately 25 years

Small carnivores

★ ★ ★ ★ ★
Serval
(Leptailurus serval)

Tierboskat (A)   Servalkatze (G)
Serval/Chat-tigre (F)   iNdlozi (Z)

The best place to see servals is along wetlands where there
is tall grass for cover and plenty of rodents for food. They
start foraging in the early evening, and are frequently still
active after sunrise. It is the tallest of the small African
cats, has long legs and is slenderly built with a long neck.

It is exceptionally quick and agile, and captures its prey
by pouncing; first locating and pinpointing the sound
made by its prey by moving its large ears, listening, and
then leaping high in the air and coming down with both
front feet on its victim. Prey includes mainly rats and mice,
but also other rodents, reptiles, birds and mammals.

Active: (☼) ☾
Shoulder height: 60cm
Mass: ♂ 11kg ♀ 9.6kg
Social structure: exclusive core territories
Collective noun: a pair of servals
Gestation: 73 days (2.4 months)
Life expectancy: approximately 12 – 17 years
Enemies: larger predators

40

Small carnivores

★ ★ ★ ★ ★

African Wild Cat
(Felis silvestris)

Vaalboskat (A)   Afrikanische Wildkatze (G)

Chat ganté (F)   iMpaka (Z)

Expect to see the African wild cat wherever mice and rats thrive, perhaps even close to lodges and in camps. When other predators are abundant, sightings will occur strictly at night. Occasionally you may find an African wild cat early morning on its way to its resting place, or sunning itself.

This is the closest relative to the domestic tabby and can easily be mistaken for it. Its long legs, bright rufous-brown, orange to chestnut markings on the back of its ears and its more upright posture when sitting, distinguish it from its domestic counterpart.

Active: ☾
Snout to tail end: ♂ 92cm ♀ 88cm
Mass: ♂ 5.1kg ♀ 4.2kg
Social structure: solitary
Collective noun: a destruction, dowt or dout of wild cats
Gestation: 65 days (two months)
Life expectancy: approximately 12–18 years
Enemies: leopard and other predators

Small carnivores

★★★★

Genet
(Genetta spp)

Muskejaatkat (A)

Ginsterkatze (G)

Genette (F)

iNsimba (Z)

During night drives, look for genets on the ground or in the trees of densely wooded areas close to water. The large-spotted genet occurs only in the higher rainfall areas and can be distinguished by the black-tipped tail. The small-spotted genet occurs virtually throughout, has an overall greyish colour, numerous spots and bars, and a white-tipped tail. They hunt in trees and on the ground, and eat rodents, insects, birds and wild fruit.

Females give birth to litters of up to three in holes or in leaf nests. When moving them, the mother carries them by the back, not the nape of the neck as other cats do. Genets are closely related to mongooses.

Large-spotted Genet:

Active: ☾   Snout to tail end: 95cm

Mass: ♂ 1.8kg ♀ 1.7kg

Social structure: solitary

Collective noun: a pair of genets

Gestation: 70–77 days (2.6 months)

Life expectancy: approximately 9–10 years

Enemies: serval, caracal, leopard, badger, nocturnal raptors

Small carnivores

Small-spotted Genet

★ ★ ★ ★ ★

African Civet
(Civettictis civetta)

Siwet (A)   Afrikanische Zibetkatze (G)
Civette d'Afrique (F)   iQaqa (Z)

This large, striking but secretive relative of the genet is common in the bushveld but rarely seen. Its habit of scavenging attracts it to places like camps and lodges where it prowls around at night, often overturning rubbish bins.

This is the only predator that seems to thrive on eating unpleasant tasting or even toxic millipedes and toads. They even consume poisonous snakes like the puffadder, but they also scavenge and supplement their diet with a variety of fruit. The musk secreted as a territorial marking has been used in the past as an ingredient of perfume.

Active: ☾
Snout to tail end: ♂ 1–1.5m
Mass: ♂ + ♀ 16–20kg
Social structure: solitary
Collective noun: a pair of civets
Gestation: about 80 days (2.7 months)
Life expectancy: approximately 15 years
Enemies: leopard and caracal, other small predators, python and raptors

46

Slender Mongoose
(Galerella sanguinea)

Swartkwasmuishond (A) Schlankmanguste (G)

Mangouste rouge (F) uChakide (Z)

This mongoose is usually seen alone and is noticed only when alarmed or when crossing the road. It can easily be confused with the dwarf mongoose, but is larger and the long tail is black-tufted. It is common and widely distributed in woodlands and wooded savannah and feeds on small vertebrates and insects.

They show an unusual social organisation in that adult

males usually live in coalitions of up to four males, much like the coalitions of lion and cheetah males. They defend a collective territory that may include several females. When they forage, they do so alone.

Active: ☀
Snout to tail end: 32cm
Mass: ♂ 715g ♀ 575g
Social structure: coalition males defend a territory with a few ♀
Collective noun: a business of mongooses
Gestation: 56–63 days (two months)
Life expectancy: approximately 15 years

tick
box

Dwarf Mongoose

Small carnivores

★★★

Banded Mongoose

★★★★

51

White-tailed Mongoose

Cape Clawless Otter

Small carnivores

Spotted-necked Otter

Honey Badger
(Mellivora capensis)

Ratel (A)

Ratel (F)

Honigdachs (G)

iNsele (Z)

Although badgers are mainly nocturnal, they are often encountered during the day. This is a tough and fearless predator that will attack any other animal it perceives as a threat, even a lion. They feed on insects, spiders, reptiles, birds, mice and rats, and will unearth any prey with their powerful forelimbs, which are adapted for digging.

Badgers are also particularly fond of honey and bee larvae. The predation on bees and its association with the greater honey guide is particularly fascinating. The bird regularly invites people and other animals such as badgers, to follow it to the nearest beehive. The co-operation offers mutual benefits.

54

Small carnivores

Active: (☼) ☾
Snout to tail end: 95cm
Mass: ♂ + ♀ 12kg
Social structure: only one partner, pair bond
Collective noun: a cete or colony of badgers
Gestation: 50–70 days (two months)
Life expectancy: approximately 24 years

★ ★ ★

Hippopotamus

(Hippopotamus amphibius)

Seekoei (A)   Flusspferd (G)

Hippopotame (F)   iMvubu (Z)

Look for hippos resting in water or basking on the bank close to their waterhole during the day. They usually have their preferred places. The water must be deep enough to cover their bodies and prevent them from overhealing. At night they are lone grazers, and consume up to 40kg per adult.

Although hippos in Africa kill more people than lions or crocodiles do, they are dangerous only when they feel threatened or their space is invaded. Their agility and speed must never be underestimated as they can run faster than humans. A threat display of yawning, showing their long razor-sharp canines, usually discourages aggressors.

Active: (☼) in water ☾ grazing
Shoulder height: ♂ 1.5m ♀ 1.44m
Mass: ♂ 1 546kg ♀ 1 385kg
♂ lower canine 22cm ♀ 14cm
Social structure: sociable groups of a ♂ and many ♀'s
Collective noun: a crash, herd, raft, pod, thunder, school, bloat or huddle of hippos
Gestation: 225–257 days (eight months)
Life expectancy: approximately 54 years

The giants

★★★★★

White Rhinoceros
(Ceratotherium simum)

Witrenoster (A)   Breitmaulnashorn (G)
Rhinocéros blanc (F)   uMkhombe (Z)

Look for white rhinos in areas that include grassland with trees, water and mud wallows. They are the second heaviest of all land mammals and spend most of their time grazing. White rhinos are rare and endangered.

There are several ways of distinguishing between the two kinds of rhino. The white rhino has a square upper lip for grazing; pointed, often tufted ears; a flattish back with a slight hump near the middle; an elongated head, which it usually holds down; the calf usually runs ahead of the mother; and when alarmed, it curls its tail and lifts it above its back.

Active: ☀ ☾
Shoulder height: ♂ 1.8m ♀ 1.7m
Mass: ♂ 2 000–2 400kg ♀ 1 600kg
Horns: two on nose, composed of hair ♂ + ♀
Social structure: solitary and territorial but occasionally in groups
Collective noun: a crash, stubbornness or herd of rhinos
Gestation: 480 days (16 months)
Life expectancy: approximately 45 years

58

The giants

★ ★ ★ ★ ★

Black Rhinoceros

(Diceros bicornis)

Swartrenoster (A) Spitzmaulnashorn (G)

Rhinocéros noir (F) uBhenjane omnyama (Z)

The black rhino is likely to be found in dense bush or thickets, since it is a browser. It also requires access to water and mud-wallowing, as well as mineral licks. Look out for black rhinos at waterholes.

The black rhino differs from its close relative by having a pointed, prehensile upper lip for browsing; rounded ears; a concave back; a rounded head, which it often holds up; and the calf usually runs behind the mother. The tail is held straight and vertical when the animal is alarmed. Lesions on the side of the body are a natural phenomenon and are caused by parasites.

Active: ☼ ☾

Shoulder height: 1.6m

Mass: ♂ 858–1 000kg ♀ 884kg

Horns: two on nose, composed of hair ♂ + ♀

Social structure: solitary, or mother and calf, not strictly territorial

Collective noun: a crash, stubbornness or herd of rhinos

Gestation: 460 days (15 months)

Life expectancy: approximately 45 years

The giants

★ ★ ★ ★ ★

African Savannah Elephant
(Loxodonta africana)

Afrika-olifant (A)   Afrikanischer Elefant (G)
Éléphant d'Afrique (F)   iNdlovu (Z)

Although they are Earth's largest land animals, they blend perfectly into the bush and can easily be passed by unnoticed. The trunk is the muscular extension of the upper lip, containing the nostrils and two fingerlike projections. They are strict vegetarians and feed on bark, roots, leaves, soft branches, grass and fruit.

When elephants approach, give them space to pass, switch off the engine and keep calm. Elephants may try to scare off intruders by kicking up dust, flapping ears, 'bush bashing', trumpeting and lifting the trunk; actions all intended to intimidate. Serious charges are silent, with ears pinned back and trunk lowered.

Active: ☀ ☾   Shoulder height: ♂ 3.45m ♀ 2.62m
Mass: ♂ 5 500–6 000kg ♀ 4 000kg
♂ + ♀ with tusks, absence usually genetic
Social structure: matriarchal clan, ♂ alone or bachelor herds
Collective noun: a herd, memory or parade of elephants
Gestation: 22 months (88 weeks)
Life expectancy: approximately 60 years

The giants

★ ★ ★ ★

Giraffe
(Giraffa camelopardalis)

Kameelperd (A)	Giraffe (G)
Girafe (F)	iNdlumanithi (Z)

Look for giraffes where there are food trees for them to browse. They are visible from afar since they are the tallest mammals and the largest ruminants. They have extremely long tongues (45cm) and can reach foliage that is beyond the reach of other browsers. Despite its great length, the giraffe's neck has just seven vertebrae like all other mammals.

Long ago, people thought a giraffe was a cross between a camel, because of the way it walked, and a leopard, because of its markings. This led to the word *camelopardalis*. The Arabs called it Zarafa and the Ethiopians Zurafa. Eventually, taxonomists named it *Giraffa camelopardalis*.

Active: ☀ (☾)
Shoulder height: ♂ 3m ♀ 2.73m
Mass: ♂ 1 192kg ♀ 828kg
Horns: conical outgrowths ♂ more pronounced than ♀
Social structure: loose groups, ♂ often solitary
Collective noun: a corps, herd, tower, stretch, journey, totter or group of giraffes
Gestation: 457 days (15.2 months)
Life expectancy: approximately 28 years

The giants

★★★★★

African Buffalo

(Syncerus caffer)

Afrika-buffel (A)　　　　　　　**Afrikanischer Büffel (G)**
Buffle d'Afrique (F)　　　　　　**iNyathi (Z)**

Buffaloes are regularly encountered on their way to water after the night feed. They require large space, are bulk grazers and feed on a variety of grasses of various lengths. They prefer open areas, are nomadic and need water every day.

The buffalo lifestyle requires vigilance of all individuals. Females need horns to defend themselves and their offspring against predators, or at least to deter them. They are bovids, which means they have a keratin sheath covering the bone of the horn, making them hollow-horned. These animals are quick-tempered and will not hesitate to use their massive horns to ram and gore if they perceive any threat.

Active: ☼ ☾
Shoulder height: ♂ 1.4m ♀ 1.4m
Mass: ♂ 590kg ♀ 513kg
Horns: ♂ broad base shielding forehead, ♀ bases not touching
Social structure: non-territorial, large mixed herds, bachelor herds, and hierarchy structure
Collective noun: a herd, troop, gang or obstinacy of buffaloes
Gestation: 343days (11.5 months)
Life expectancy: approximately 25 years

The giants

★★
Plains Zebra
(Equus quagga)

Bontsebra (A)   Steppenzebra (G)
Zèbre de Burchell (F)   iDube (Z)

Look for zebra on grasslands, plains and open or lightly wooded areas, close to water. The males and females look alike and are often found in large aggregations at water-holes. Note that the lower legs and belly have no stripes and that shadow stripes occur between the black stripes. No two zebras have exactly the same stripe pattern.

Zebras usually rest in pairs with their heads placed on the other's back, facing in opposite directions. This enables a pair to watch for danger in all directions and brush flies off each other's face.

Active: ☀ ☾
Shoulder height: ♂ 1.3m ♀ 1.3m
Mass: ♂ 313kg ♀ 302kg
Social structure: gregarious, non-territorial, small family groups
Collective noun: a zeal, cohort, dazzle or herd of zebras
Gestation: 360–390 days (12–13 months)
Life expectancy: approximately 35 years
Enemies: lion, hyena and wild dog

The giants

★★

Greater Kudu

(Tragelaphus strepsiceros)

Koedoe (A)   **Großer Kudu (G)**

Grand Koudou (F)   **uMgankla/iMbodwane (Z)**

Kudus are found in places where there is dense cover, such as scrubby woodland. They prefer rocky, broken terrain. They are browsers and are well concealed by their colouring. The males of this second-tallest of antelope have the most spectacular horns, while the smaller females are hornless. They display the huge cupped ears of the species to best advantage.

Despite being long and twisted, the horns never get in the way when the antelope flees from predators. It simply lifts its chin so that the horns lie flat at shoulder level. They are high jumpers, clearing fences up to 2.5m high.

Active: ☀ ☾
Shoulder height: 1.45m
Mass: ♂ 220kg ♀ 152kg
Horns: only ♂ corkscrew twisted, long
Social structure: gregarious, small herds
Collective noun: a cluster or herd of kudus
Gestation: 270 days (nine months)
Life expectancy: approximately 11 years
Enemies: leopard, wild dog, cheetah and lion

Antelopes

Female

★ ★ ★ ★ ★

Eland
(Tragelaphus oryx)

Eland (A)

Éland du Cap (F)

Elenantilope (G)

iMpofu (Z)

It is difficult to predict where this antelope will be found since it has such a nomadic lifestyle. It is one of the most adaptable of all antelope and is the largest one in Africa, weighing up to a tonne or more. The characteristic dewlap is enormous, and bearded in the males.

It has a cloven hoof, which is well adapted for its nomadic lifestyle of covering long distances. Owing to the animal's springy gait, massive weight, and the hoof design, the hoof splays out when walking and snaps shut when the foot is lifted, causing an audible click.

Active: ☼ ☾

Shoulder height: 1.7m

Mass: ♂ 1 034kg ♀ 700kg

Horns: both, spiral, ♂ much larger than ♀

Social structure: big herds up to 500 strong

Collective noun: a herd of eland

Gestation: 274 days (8–9 months)

Life expectancy: approximately 12 years

Enemies: lion and wild dog; the young are predated by leopard, hyena, cheetah

72

Antelopes

★ ★ ★
Nyala
(Tragelaphus angasii)

Njala (A)   Tieflandnyala (G)
Nyala (F)   iNyala (Z)

Nyalas are common only in the Zululand bushveld and the north-eastern parts of southern Africa. You will find this close relative of the bushbuck in thickets and dense woodland, generally near water. It browses on leaves, feeds on pods, fruits, herbs and also on fresh green grass.

The colour of the male coat differs considerably from that of the female, and becomes darker as it matures. The dominance display of a male is spectacular. It struts with mane erect and neck arched, and presents its flank to the rival, making itself appear bigger. The tail is raised over the rump and the white hairs fan out; the head is lowered and the horns point outward.

Active: (☼) ☾
Shoulder height: 106cm
Mass: ♂ 106kg ♀ 60kg
Horns: only ♂ with twisted horns
Social structure: gregarious, not territorial,
♀ with last few offspring, ♂ in small groups
Collective noun: a cluster of nyalas
Gestation: 220 days (seven months)
74 Life expectancy: approximately nine years

Antelopes

Female

★ ★ ★
Bushbuck
(Tragelaphus scriptus)

Bosbok (A)   Buschbock/Schirrantilope (G)
Guib harnachée (F)   uNkonka (Z)

Look for the bushbuck along forest edges and dense-ly vegetated places near water. Along the Zambezi and Chobe rivers, bushbuck are more reddish in colour with more prominent white markings than elsewhere. They are browsers, but also feed on seeds, fruits, flowers and tender green grass.

This solitary antelope is neither territorial, nor does it defend its home range. The stripes and spots on its coat help with camouflage, blending it perfectly with the dappled shade of its surroundings. Cornered bushbuck males can be extremely dangerous, using their sharp horns and hooves to good effect. An enraged bushbuck can even scare off leopard.

Active: (☼) ☾
Shoulder height: ♂ 79cm ♀ 69cm
Mass: ♂ 40–80kg ♀ 30–60kg
Horns: only ♂ with twisted horns
Social structure: ♂ solitary ♀ solitary or with a young
Collective noun: a cluster of bushbucks
Gestation: 180 days (six months)
Life expectancy: approximately nine years

Antelopes

Female

★

Impala
(Aepyceros melampus)

Rooibok (A)   Impala/Schwarzfersenantilope (G)
Impala (F)   iMpala (Z)

Impalas will probably be the first game species you encounter on your visit as they are abundant and by far the commonest animals in bushveld reserves. They are grazers and/or browsers, depending on the habitat, but prefer open woodland.

The black tufts on the rear feet above the hooves are scent glands. Adult males also have scent glands on the face, which the dominant males often use to mark their territories and advertise their presence by rubbing scent on to the trunks of trees and other vegetation. During the rutting season, there is much roaring and aggression among the males as they fight for dominance.

Active: ☼
Shoulder height: ♂ 90cm ♀ 89cm
Mass: ♂ 44kg ♀ 40kg
Horns: only ♂
Social structure: territorial ♂ + breeding herd; bachelor herd
Collective noun: a herd or rank of impalas
Gestation: 196 days (6.5 months)
78 Life expectancy: unknown

Antelopes

Female

★
Blue Wildebeest
(Connochaetes taurinus)

Blouwildebees (A)   Streifengnu (G)

Gnou bleu/à queue noire (F)   iNkonkoni (Z)

You will find these animals in small or large herds on short-grass plains and acacia savannah. The blue wildebeests, with their blunt muzzles and wide row of incisors, prefer short grasses. Unfortunately, they cannot reach these unless they are exposed and therefore they can be seen following zebras, which graze medium-height grasses, exposing the short grasses.

Scent-marking is important for territorial species such as wildebeest. The pre-orbital gland is situated between the eye and the nose, and is rubbed against twigs, stems, grass stalks or trees to communicate by scent with other members of the species.

Active: ☀ ☾
Shoulder height: ♂ 1.74m ♀ 1.35m
Mass: ♂ 249.8kg ♀ 182.7kg
Horns: ♂ well-developed bosses, ♀ lighter in build
Social structure: gregarious, big herds, territorial ♂,
♀ herds, bachelor groups
Collective noun: a herd or implausibility of wildebeests
Gestation: 250 days (8.4 months)

80

Antelopes

★★★★

Tsessebe
(Damaliscus lunatus)

Basterhartbees/Tsessebe (A)   **Leierantilope (G)**
Damalisque (F)

This antelope occurs only in the far north-east of South Africa, and in Botswana and Zimbabwe where there are medium-length grasslands and transitional zones between woodland and grassland. It selects the greenest, most tender growth, avoiding mature stems and dry grass.

   Its lean body is built for speed, and the tsessebe is considered the fastest antelope in southern Africa. Its habit of 'mud-packing', where it digs its horns into muddy patches while it is on its knees, possibly serves to make the horns look more formidable when caked with mud. Both sexes will do this.

Active: ☀ ☾
Shoulder height: ♂ 1.26m ♀ 1.25m
Mass: ♂ 130kg ♀ 108kg
Horns: ♂ + ♀ with horns
Social structure: all forms of territorial behaviour
Collective noun: a herd or cluster of tsessebes
Gestation: eight months
Life expectancy: approximately nine years
Enemies: lion, leopard, wild dog and hyena

82

Antelopes

Roan Antelope
(Hippotragus equinus)

Bastergemsbok (A)   Pferdeantilope (G)

Antilope rouanne (F)   iNoni (Z)

Although the roan antelope is widespread, it is rarely seen. As a grazer and browser, it tolerates taller grass, unlike its close relative the sable. It prefers wetter parts with broad-leafed deciduous woodland, and floodplains. It is sensitive to habitat change and very specific about its requirements, which results in a discontinuous occurrence in southern Africa.

The head, with extraordinarily large ears, has black and white markings that resemble a mask. Their sense of hearing is very acute, and any noise makes them extremely skittish. The roan is the second heaviest antelope after the eland.

Active: ☀ ☾

Shoulder height: ♂ 1.4m ♀ 1.2m

Mass: ♂ 270kg ♀ 260kg

Horns: ♂ + ♀ curved backwards

Social structure: small to medium herds

Collective noun: a cluster of roan antelopes

Gestation: 276–287 days (9–9.5 months)

Life expectancy: approximately 19 years

★★★★★

Sable Antelope

(Hippotragus niger)

Swartwitpens (A)   Rappenantilope (G)

Hippotrague noir (F)   iMpapalampala (Z)

Finding sable is always a special sighting. It prefers savannah woodland with grassland and widely spaced, broadleafed, deciduous, fire-resistant trees. It occurs in the northern parts of southern Africa. A grazer and browser, it needs water at least every other day.

Sable antelopes are regarded as one of the most handsome antelope with the longest horns of all species, except the kudu. Most predators are extremely wary of the long impressive backward curving horns. When threatened it backs into bushes, drops to its knees and scythes the air from side to side with its horns to deter predators.

Active: ☼ ☾
Shoulder height: ♂ 1.4m ♀ 1.17m
Mass: ♂ 230kg ♀ 220kg
Horns: both, but ♂ massive, sable like, curled backwards, longer than in ♀
Social structure: herds, ♀ and young with territorial ♂
Collective noun: a herd or cluster of sable antelopes
Gestation: 266 days (8–9 months)
Life expectancy: approximately nine years

86

Female

★★
Waterbuck
(Kobus ellipsiprymnus)

Waterbok/Kringgat (A)   **Ellypsen-Wasserbock (G)**
Cobe à croissant (F)   **iPhiva (Z)**

Look for waterbuck in grassland at the edges of savannah woodland, close to wetlands and water. It is a grazer of medium and short grasses and browses on foliage when green grass is not available.

   The white ring around the rump probably serves as a following mechanism; each animal follows the signal of the animal in front, and in turn serves as a following beacon for the one behind. Abundant sweat glands secrete a musky substance, which taints the flesh and gives it an unpleasant flavour that effectively deters predators and other hunters.

Active: ☀ ☾
Shoulder height: 1.3m
Mass: ♂ 270kg ♀ 250kg
Horns: only ♂, large, slightly but sweepingly curled forward
Social structure: social and occur in groups, dominant males territorial
Collective noun: a herd or cluster of waterbucks
Gestation: 280 days (8.5–9 months)
Life expectancy: approximately 12 years

88

Antelopes

Female

★ ★ ★ ★ ★

Southern Reedbuck

(Redunca arundinum)

Rietbok (A)   Großriedbock (G)

Cobe des roseaux (F)   Mziki (Z)

Reedbucks can be found where there are stands of high grass or reedbeds near water. They depend on the existence of wetlands, vleis and seasonally moist grasslands.

Reedbucks have a distinctive voice. When disturbed they give a characteristic piercing whistle and run in a distinctive rocking canter, displaying their white tail, and whistling at every bound. The clicking sound is caused by forced expulsion of breath through the nostrils, varying in pitch and tone. In distress, the voice is a long-drawn plaintive cry, but when suddenly frightened, it makes a soft hissing sound.

Active: (☼) ☾
Shoulder height: ♂ 0.9m ♀ 0.8m
Mass: ♂ 70kg ♀ 51kg
Horns: only ♂
Social structure: not gregarious but form pairs or family groups
Collective noun: a cluster or pair of reedbucks
Gestation: 225 days (eight months)
Life expectancy: approximately nine years

Antelopes

Female

Suni/Livingstone's Antelope

(Neotragus moschatus)

Soenie (A)

Antilope musquée/Suni (F)

Moschusböckchen/Suni (G)

iNhlengane (Z)

This is a rare antelope found only in the far northern parts of the Limpopo province, Mozambique, and in the scarce sand forests of Maputaland. It prefers dry woodland with dense undergrowth. Suni are shy and wary, feeding on herbs, low shrubs, fruit and mushrooms.

This is a small antelope; only the blue duiker is smaller. They use their well-developed pre-orbital glands for marking their territories, and they also use communal middens. They have the largest pre-orbital scent glands, relative to size, of all antelope. To see a suni on a game drive is indeed a special sighting.

Antelopes

Active: ☀ ☾   Shoulder height: 35cm

Mass: ♂ 5kg ♀ 5.4kg

Horns: only ♂, straight, strongly ridged

Social structure: solitary, territorial, also occur in small groups

Collective noun: a pair of suni antelopes

Gestation: 172–192 days (six months)

Life expectancy: unknown

★ ★ ★ ★ ★

Sharpe's Grysbok
(Raphicerus sharpei)

Sharpe se grysbok (A)   Sharpes Greisbock (G)
Grysbok de Sharpe (F)

This small antelope is found in the north-eastern savannah regions of southern Africa, in areas with low shrubs and grass. It is nocturnal, shy and secretive. It is easily overlooked and extremely rare. Look for it in rocky, hilly areas of mopane veld where there are no dense stands of grass.

The coat is rich reddish-brown and suffused with long greyish hairs, which distinguishes it clearly from the steenbok. They are not only prey to the larger diurnal and nocturnal predators such as lions and leopards, but are also preyed upon by pythons and large raptors.

Active: (☀) ☾
Shoulder height: 45cm
Mass: ♂ 7.7kg ♀ 7.3kg
Horns: only ♂ short, straight
Social structure: solitary, pairs or ♀ with offspring
Collective noun: a pair of grysbokke
Gestation: 210 days (seven months)
Life expectancy: unknown
Enemies: leopard, eagle and caracal

Antelopes

Klipspringer
(Oreotragus oreotragus)

Klipspringer/Klipbokkie (A)   Klippspringer (G)
Oréotrague (F)   iGogo (Z)

This sure-footed antelope lives on rocky outcrops and in mountainous areas (koppies) and is independent of drinking-water sources. A browser, it feeds on leaves, shoots, berries, pods, flowers and succulents. When you see one, look for its mate, for it will almost certainly be close by. They form lifelong pair-bonds.

The specialised hooves have flat tips, which enable it to bound up and down steep slopes. It can jump from rock to rock, landing on all fours on a small space. The hairs are hollow, flattened and spiny, springy in texture and adhere loosely to the skin. In bygone days, klipspringer hair was sought after for saddle stuffing because of these unique features.

Active:
Shoulder height: 60cm
Mass: ♂ 10.6kg ♀ 13.2kg
Horns: only ♂, vertical upward, slight forward curve
Social structure: in pairs, or pair with offspring or solitary
Collective noun: a pair or family group of klipspringers
Gestation: estimated at 150–225 days (5–7.5 months)
Life expectancy: unknown

Antelopes

★★
Steenbok/Steinbuck
(Raphicerus campestris)

Steenbok (A)

Steinböckchen (G)

Steenbok (F)

iQhina (Z)

This tiny antelope is common in the open and dry bush-veld. It is not dependent on water sources, since it obtains sufficient moisture from its diet of foliage, seedpods and seeds, berries and tender green grass. Sexcs are alike, except for the horns.

Both sexes are territorial and defend their areas against others. They use dung middens. When about to urinate or defecate, the antelope prepares a slight depression with its front hooves, in which it leaves a deposit and then covers it up. When they sense danger, they hide in the grass by lying flat to escape detection, not moving unless they are flushed out.

Active: ☼ ☾
Shoulder height: 50cm
Mass: ♂ 10.9kg ♀ 11.3kg
Horns: only ♂ short and straight
Social structure: solitary, territorial
Collective noun: a pair of steenbokke/steinbucks
Gestation: 168–173 days (5.6 months)
Life expectancy: approximately nine years

Antelopes

★★★

Common/Grey Duiker
(Sylvicapra grimmia)

Gewone duiker (A)
Céphalophe couronné (F)

Kronenducker (G)
iMpunzi (Z)

Look for duikers in areas with ample shrubs and other plants growing under trees. This is one of the most common small antelope in the bushveld and the last to be eliminated by settlements. Its diel is varied but it eats mainly herbs, fruits, seeds and cultivated crops.

They are secretive and, if disturbed, will steal away with head lowered and tail up. When they suddenly decide to flee, they seem to dash between hiding places, almost diving into thickets. *'Duiker'* is the Afrikaans word for diver. Both sexes have a characteristic spiky tuft of hair between the ears.

Active: ☼ ☾
Shoulder height: 50cm
Mass: ♂ 16.2kg ♀ 16.7kg
Horns: ♂ short and straight, ♀ absent or stunted
Social structure: usually solitary
Collective noun: a pair of duikers
Gestation: 191 days (6.3 months)
Life expectancy: approximately nine years
Enemies: many, including large and smaller predators, crocodile, python and large birds of prey

Antelopes

★★★★★

Red Duiker
(Cephalophus natalensis)

Rooiduiker (A)   Rotducker (G)
Céphalophe du Natal (F)   uMsumpe/uMkhumbi (Z)

This tiny, beautiful antelope is extremely scarce in the Greater Kruger. It occurs along subtropical forested areas near water, where it browses primarily on fallen leaves, flowers and fruit, as well as the fine stems of shrubs. It is more common in the Zululand parks.

Although solitary, individuals do occasionally meet. They may greet each other by rubbing the scent glands in front of their eyes together. They also mark their home ranges by frequently rubbing their scent glands on branches, twigs and tree trunks.

Active:
Shoulder height: ♂ 41–43cm ♀ 41cm
Mass: ♂ 11.7kg ♀ 11.9kg
Horns: ♂ + ♀ with short straight horns
Social structure: solitary or ♀ with offspring, ♂ territorial
Collective noun: a pair of duikers
Gestation: 210 days (seven months)
Life expectancy: approximately nine years
Enemies: many, including large and smaller predators, crocodile, python and large birds of prey

Antelopes

★ ★ ★ ★ ★

Aardvark/Antbear
(Orycteropus afer)

Erdvark (A)   Erdferkel (G)
Oryctérope (F)   iSambane (Z)

The aardvark starts foraging late at night and is therefore seldom seen on drives. Although these animals have pig-like snouts, they are not related to pigs at all. They use their powerful forelegs to excavate burrows where they live, and also to excavate the nests of formicid ants and, to a lesser extent, termites.

The aardvark locates its food source by its acute sense of smell complemented by a good sense of hearing. Their large ears are movable and help to detect movement and the presence of danger. Their eyesight, however, is extremely poor.

Active: (☼) ☾
Snout to tail end: ♂ 1.7m ♀ 1.5m
Mass: ♂ 45kg ♀ 41kg
Social structure: solitary
Collective noun: an armoury of aardvarks
Gestation: 243 days (eight months)
Life expectancy: approximately 10 years
Enemies: all big predators, python

Other mammals

Common Warthog
(Phacochoerus africanus)

Vlakvark (A)	**Warzenschwein (G)**
Phacochère (F)	**iNtibane (Z)**

Look for warthogs on floodplains, open areas, dry pans and around waterholes. They avoid dense cover and favour open short grassland with edible grasses, rhizomes, bulbs and tubers. Warthogs drop down on the knees of their forelegs to dig more effectively, using their snouts. They do not depend on water sources, but nevertheless drink fairly regularly and enjoy mud-wallowing.

The warthog's foremost enemies are the lion and leopard. They defend themselves with their long canines called tushes. The lower ones are razor sharp and slightly curved but shorter than the upper ones, against which they are honed when the animal eats.

Active: ☀

Shoulder height: ♂ 68cm ♀ 60cm

Mass: ♂ 79kg ♀ 66kg

Warts: ♂ two pairs of warts on face, ♀ one pair

Social structure: sows live in clans with young, no territorialism

Collective noun: a sounder or clan of warthogs

Gestation: 164–182 days (5.5–6 months)

Life expectancy: approximately 20 years

Other mammals

★ ★ ★ ★ ★

Bushpig
(Potamochoerus larvatus)

Bosvark (A)   Buschschwein (G)

Potamochère (F)   iNgulube (Z)

Look out for bushpigs in riverine vegetation where there are dense thickets or tall grass for cover. They are shy and highly nocturnal animals, seldom seen during the day. They eat virtually anything from plant matter, insects and worms, and occasionally even feed on carrion.

Bushpigs do not drop to their knees when rooting plants as warthogs do, nor do they have warts. Unlike warthogs, they run with their tails down, and their tushes (tusks) are inconspicuous. Like warthogs, they enjoy mud-wallowing, probably to get rid of insects and for temperature control. They are aggressive and dangerous and their sharp tusks can inflict serious wounds.

Active: (☼) ☾

Shoulder height: 70cm

Mass: ♂ 72kg ♀ 68kg

Social structure: only one partner, gregarious but not territorial

Collective noun: a sounder of bushpigs

Gestation: 119 days (four months)

Life expectancy: approximately 20 years

Other mammals

Ground Pangolin

(Manis temminckii)

Ietermagog (A)   Steppenschuppentier (G)
Pangolin de Temminck (F)

Look for pangolins on floodplain grasslands and rocky slopes where the soil is sandy. They feed mainly on ants and termites, using the claws on their forefeet to open underground food sources, and lick up ants and termites with their long sticky tongue. Pangolins have no teeth and the food is ground up in the muscular part of the stomach, aided by grit.

Pangolins are armoured with heavy yellow-brown scales. They walk on their hind legs with the tail off the ground, forelegs and head just above the ground. They defend themselves simply by rolling into a ball when threatened and are thus seldom preyed upon.

Active: (☼) ☾
Snout to tail end: ♂ 1m ♀ 0.9m
Mass: ♂ 13.3kg ♀ 7.4kg
♂ + ♀ similar in appearance
Social structure: solitary
Collective noun: a pair of pangolins
Gestation: 139 days (4.7 months)
Life expectancy: approximately 12 years

Other mammals

112

Tree Squirrel ★★

Other mammals

113

Porcupine ★★★

Chacma Baboon
(Papio ursinus)

tick box

Bobbejaan (A)   Pavian (G)

Chacma (F)   iMfene (Z)

This species occurs throughout southern Africa's savannah areas, wherever there is water and secure sleeping places. Baboons are easy to spot as the troop moves from its sleeping trec to foraging grounds. They eat almost anything; grasses, seeds, flowers, fruits, tubers and bulbs, insects, frogs, reptiles, eggs and even small mammals.

When a troop is feeding or on the move, certain individuals, usually males, will climb on to vantage points to scan the environment for potential danger. Loud barking is usually an alarm call that warns the troop of danger. These lookouts also help to protect the juveniles by keeping them from straying.

Active: ☀

Shoulder height: 75cm

Mass: ♂ 22–32kg ♀ 14–16kg

Social structure: live in mixed troops and have a complex society

Collective noun: a flange, troup, troop, tribe, congress or rumpus of baboons

Gestation: 183 days (six months)

Life expectancy: approximately 30–45 years

Other mammals

★★

Vervet Monkey
(Cercophitecus pygerythrus)

Blou-aap (A)

Vervet (F)

Grüne Meerkatze (G)

iNkawu (Z)

Monkeys are generally found in vegetation close to streams or rivers. They live in troops of family groups, favouring areas with trees for shelter, and eat mostly plant material. They also eat insects, lizards, birds' eggs and nestlings.

The troop has a dominant male that maintains his status with grimacing and threatening gestures. Grooming is a way of cleaning and neatening the fur, getting rid of big ticks, scabs, flakes of skin and salty deposits caused by perspiration. But the activity is also a way of building bonds and alliances between individuals, and reinforcing hierarchies.

Active: ☀
Snout to tail end: ♂ 114cm ♀ 102cm
Mass: ♂ 5.5kg ♀ 4kg
♂ with vivid genital colouring
Social structure: gregarious with a clear order of dominance within the troop
Collective noun: a shrewdness, cartload, tribe, troup or troop of monkeys
Gestation: 165 days (5.5 months)
Life expectancy: approximately 30 years

Other mammals

Lesser Galago/Bushbaby
(Galago moholi)

Nagapie (A)   Moholi/Kleiner Galago (G)
Petit galago (F)   siNkwe (Z)

Look for this tiny primate in woodland with typical acacia stands. Acacias are a source of gum and have a rich insect life, both important food items for the bushbaby. Its eyes are noticeably large in relation to its head.

It lives in the dense canopies of trees, resting during the day in groups of up to six on a platform-like nest. It sleeps curled up on its side, covered by its tail. The nests are constructed from leaves or tangles of vegetation in the holes of trees. It is extremely agile and able to leap a few metres at a time. On the ground it hops, using its hind legs only.

Active: ☾
Snout to tail end: 37cm
Mass: ♂ 165g ♀ 150g
Social structure: small groups
Collective noun: a group of galagos
Gestation: 121–124 days (four months)
Life expectancy: approximately 14 years
Enemies: nocturnal raptors, genet and python

Other mammals

Thick-tailed Bushbaby

(Otolemur crassicaudatus)

Bosnagaap (A)   Riesengalago (G)

Galago à queue épaisse (F)   siNkwe (Z)

This animal is associated with well-developed woodland where there is tree gum to be found. It is often heard in rest camps at night. Its raucous, crow-like cries attract attention, not only from their own companions, but also from rivals. It rests in nests in trees during the day and emerges after sunset, first to groom and then to forage.

Their eyes are smaller in relation to their head size than the lesser galago, but also shine brightly in the darkness with a reddish glow if they are caught in a beam of light. They run along branches, with short jumps where necessary. On the ground, they move on all fours with hindquarters and the tail held high.

Active: ☾
Snout to tail end: ♂ 71cm ♀ 58cm
Mass: ♂ 1.2kg ♀ 0.74kg
Social structure: stable groups
Collective noun: a group of galagos
Gestation: 132–135 days (more than four months)
Life expectancy: approximately 15 years
Enemies: nocturnal raptors, genet and python

Other mammals

★★★

Nile Crocodile
(Crocodylus niloticus)

Krokodil (A)   Krokodil (G)

Crocodile (F)   iNgwenja (Z)

Crocodiles are reptiles and easy to see when sunning themselves on riverbanks. They are cold-blooded and need to absorb heat from the sun. Their ability to lie concealed with most of their body underwater, combined with their speed over short distances, makes them effective opportunistic hunters of larger prey. They grab such prey in their powerful jaws, drag it into the water, and hold it under until it drowns.

Eggs are laid in sand on sunny riverbanks and are incubated by the sun. The sex of the hatchlings depends on the incubation temperature; females are produced at low temperatures and males at higher temperatures.

Active: ☼ basking in sun ☾ under water
Snout to tail end: ♂ 2.5–3.9m (can be up to 6m)
Mass: ♂ 450–600kg
Amphibious, communal, parents look after nests
Collective noun: a congregation, float, bask or nest of crocodiles
Gestation: 16–80 eggs are laid and hatch within 85 days
Life expectancy: approximately 45 years

Reptiles

Water Monitor

Reptiles

★★★★★

African Python

★★★

Puff Adder

Crested Guineafowl
Kuifkoptarentaal

Helmeted Guineafowl
Gewone Tarentaal

Common Ostrich
Volstruis

Greater Flamingo
Grootflamink

Lesser Flamingo
Kleinflamink

☐ Harlequin Quail
Bontkwartel

☐ Coqui Francolin
Swempie

☐ Crested Francolin
Bospatrys

☐ Shelley's Francolin
Laeveldpatrys

☐ Natal Spurfowl
Natalse Fisant

☐ Swainson's Spurfowl
Bosveldfisant

127

Southern Pochard
Bruineend

African Black Duck
Swarteend

Fulvous Whistling Duck
Fluiteend

Knob-billed Duck
Knobbeleend

White-backed Duck
Witrugeend

White-faced
Whistling Duck
Nonnetjie-eend

☐ Yellow-billed Duck
Geelbekwitreier

♂ ♀ African Pygmy Goose
Dwerggans

☐ Egyptian Goose
Kolgans

☐ Spur-winged Goose
Wildemakou

☐ Hottentot Teal
Gevlekte Eend

☐ Red-billed Teal
Rooibekeend

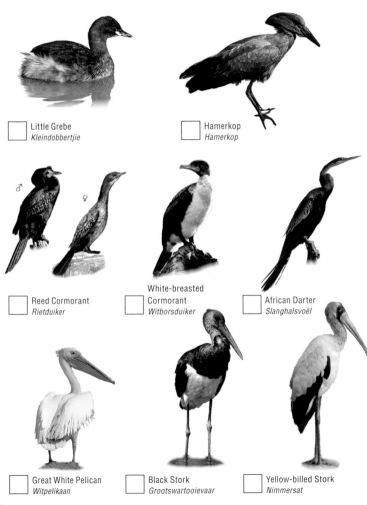

Little Grebe
Kleindobbertjie

Hamerkop
Hamerkop

Reed Cormorant
Rietduiker

White-breasted
Cormorant
Witborsduiker

African Darter
Slanghalsvoël

Great White Pelican
Witpelikaan

Black Stork
Grootswartooievaar

Yellow-billed Stork
Nimmersat

African Openbill
Oopbekooievaar

Abdim's Stork
Kleinswartooievaar

Marabou Stork
Maraboe

Saddle-billed Stork
Saalbekooievaar

White Stork
Witooievaar

Woolly-necked Stork
Wolnekooievaar

☐ Black-crowned
Night-Heron
Gewone Nagreier

☐ Green-backed Heron
Groenrugreier

☐ Squacco Heron
Ralreier

☐ Black Heron
Swartreier

☐ Goliath Heron
Reusereier

☐ Black-headed Heron
Swartkopreier

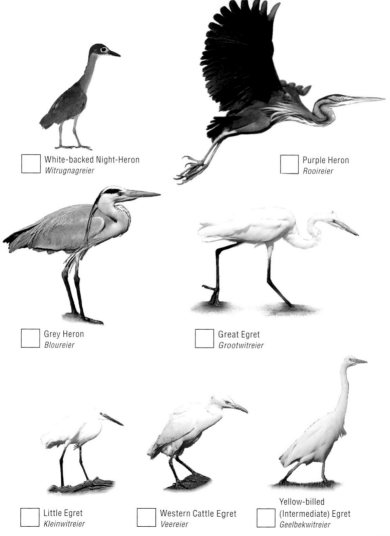

☐ White-backed Night-Heron
Witrugnagreier

☐ Purple Heron
Rooireier

☐ Grey Heron
Bloureier

☐ Great Egret
Grootwitreier

☐ Little Egret
Kleinwitreier

☐ Western Cattle Egret
Veereier

Yellow-billed
(Intermediate) Egret
☐ *Geelbekwitreier*

133

☐ Dwarf Bittern
Dwergrietreier

☐ Little Bittern
Kleinrietreier

☐ Hadeda Ibis
Hadeda

☐ Glossy Ibis
Glansibis

☐ African Sacred Ibis
Skoorsteenveer

☐ African Spoonbill
Lepelaar

Western Osprey
Visvalk

Shikra
Gebande Sperwer

African Marsh Harrier
Afrikaanse Vleivalk

Montagu's Harrier
Blouvleivalk

Secretarybird
Sekretarisvoël

Pallid Harrier
Witborsvleivalk

135

African Cuckoo Hawk
Koekoekvalk

African Harrier-Hawk
Kaalwangvalk

Black Kite
Swartwou

Bat Hawk
Vlermuisvalk

Black-shouldered Kite
Blouvalk

Yellow-billed Kite
Geelbekwou

☐ Dickinson's Kestrel
Dickinsongrysvalk

☐ Bateleur
Berghaan

☐ Common (Steppe) Buzzard
Bruinjakkalsvoël

☐ European Honey Buzzard
Wespedief

☐ Jackal Buzzard
Rooiborsjakkalsvoël

☐ Lizard Buzzard
Akkedisvalk

137

☐ African Goshawk
Afrikaanse Sperwer

☐ Dark Chanting Goshawk
Dunkersingvalk

☐ Gabar Goshawk
Witkruissperwer/klein singvalk

☐ African Fish Eagle
Visarend

☐ African Hawk Eagle
Grootjagarend

☐ Ayres's Hawk Eagle
Kleinjagarend

Black-chested
Snake Eagle
Swartborsslangarend

Booted Eagle
Dwergarend

Brown Snake Eagle
Bruinslangarend

Crowned Eagle
Kroonarend

Lesser Spotted Eagle
Gevlekte Arend

Long-crested Eagle
Langkuifarend

Martial Eagle
Breekoparend

Steppe Eagle
Steppe - Arend

Tawny Eagle
Roofarend

Verreauxs' Eagle
Witkruisarend

Wahlberg's Eagle
Bruinarend

Black Sparrowhawk
Swartsperwer

140

Little Sparrowhawk
Kleinsperwer

Ovambo Sparrowhawk
Ovambomsperwer

Red-crested Korhaan
Boskorhaan

Black-bellied Bustard
Langbeenkorhaan

Kori Bustard
Gompou

Egyptian Vulture
Egiptiese Aasvoël

Hooded Vulture
Monnikaasvoël

Palm-nut Vulture
Witaasvoël

Cape
Vulture
Kransaasvoël

Lappet-faced
Vulture
Swartaasvoël

White-headed Vulture
Witkopaasvoël

White-backed Vulture
Witrugaasvoël

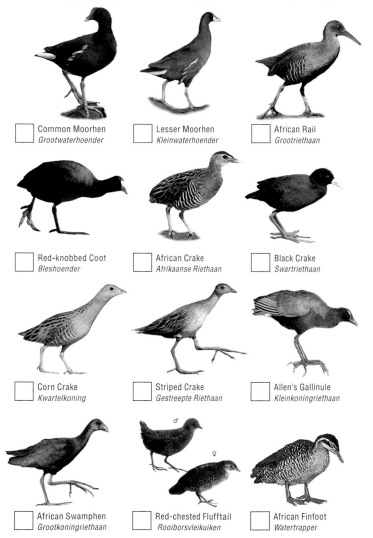

☐ Common Moorhen
Grootwaterhoender

☐ Lesser Moorhen
Kleinwaterhoender

☐ African Rail
Grootriethaan

☐ Red-knobbed Coot
Bleshoender

☐ African Crake
Afrikaanse Riethaan

☐ Black Crake
Swartriethaan

☐ Corn Crake
Kwartelkoning

☐ Striped Crake
Gestreepte Riethaan

☐ Allen's Gallinule
Kleinkoningriethaan

☐ African Swamphen
Grootkoningriethaan

☐ Red-chested Flufftail
Rooiborsvleikuiken

☐ African Finfoot
Watertrapper

143

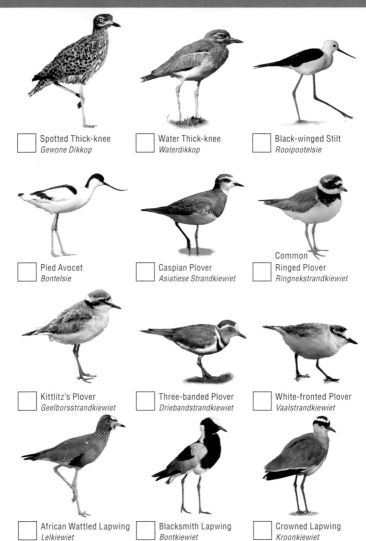

☐ Spotted Thick-knee
Gewone Dikkop

☐ Water Thick-knee
Waterdikkop

☐ Black-winged Stilt
Rooipootelsie

☐ Pied Avocet
Bontelsie

☐ Caspian Plover
Asiatiese Strandkiewiet

☐ Common
Ringed Plover
Ringnekstrandkiewiet

☐ Kittlitz's Plover
Geelborsstrandkiewiet

☐ Three-banded Plover
Driebandstrandkiewiet

☐ White-fronted Plover
Vaalstrandkiewiet

☐ African Wattled Lapwing
Lelkiewiet

☐ Blacksmith Lapwing
Bontkiewiet

☐ Crowned Lapwing
Kroonkiewiet

144

Senegal Lapwing
Kleinswartvlerkkiewiet

White-crowned Lapwing
Witkopkiewiet

Greater Painted-Snipe
Goudsnip

African Jacana
Grootlangtoon

Lesser Jacana
Dwerglangtoon

Ruff
Kemphaan

Common Sandpiper
Gewone Ruiter

Curlew Sandpiper
Krombekstrandloper

Green Sandpiper
Witgatruiter

Marsh Sandpiper
Moerasruiter

Wood Sandpiper
Bosruiter

Common Greenshank
Groenpootruiter

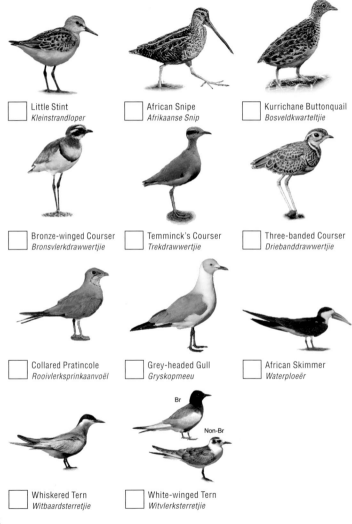

Little Stint
Kleinstrandloper

African Snipe
Afrikaanse Snip

Kurrichane Buttonquail
Bosveldkwarteltjie

Bronze-winged Courser
Bronsvlerkdrawwertjie

Temminck's Courser
Trekdrawwertjie

Three-banded Courser
Driebanddrawwertjie

Collared Pratincole
Rooivlerksprinkaanvoël

Grey-headed Gull
Gryskopmeeu

African Skimmer
Waterploeër

Whiskered Tern
Witbaardsterretjie

White-winged Tern
Witvlerksterretjie

Br

Non-Br

Eurasian Hobby
Europese Boomvalk

Lesser Kestrel
Kleinrooivalk

Rock Kestrel
Kransvalk

Amur Falcon
Oostelike Rooipootvalk

Lanner Falcon
Edelvalk

Peregrine Falcon
Swerfvalk

Red-footed Falcon
Westelike Rooipootvalk

Sooty Falcon
Roetvalk

Double-banded Sandgrouse
Dubbelbandsandpatrys

147

☐ African Green Pigeon
Papcgaaiduif

☐ Speckled Pigeon
Kransduif

☐ African Mourning Dove
Rooioogtortelduif

☐ Cape Turtle-Dove
Gewone Tortelduif

☐ Emerald-spotted Wood-Dove
Groenvlekduifie

☐ Laughing Dove
Rooiborsduifie

☐ Namaqua Dove
Namakwaduifie

☐ Red-eyed Dove
Grootringduif

☐ Tambourine Dove
Witborsduifie

Brown-headed Parrot
Bruinkoppapegaai

Grey-headed Parrot
Savannepapegaai

Meyer's Parrot
Bosveldpapegaai

Grey
Go-away-bird
Kwêvoël

Purple-crested
Turaco
Bloukuifloerie

Black Coucal
Swartvleiloerie

Burchell's Coucal
Gewone Vleiloerie

Senegal Coucal
Senegalvleiloerie

African
Cuckoo
Afrikaanse Koekoek

Black
Cuckoo
Swartkoekoek

Common
Cuckoo
Europese Koekoek

♂ ♀
Diederik
Cuckoo
Diederikkie

Great
Spotted Cuckoo
Gevlekte Koekoek

Jacobin
Cuckoo
Bontnuwejaarsvoël

Klaas's Cuckoo
Meitjie

Levaillant's
Cuckoo
Gestreepte Nuwejaarsvoël

Red-chested
Cuckoo
Piet-My-Vrou

Thick-billed
Cuckoo
Dikbekkoekoek

151

African Grass Owl
Grasuil

African Scops Owl
Skopsuil / Witwanguil

African Wood Owl
Bosuil

Marsh Owl
Vlei-Uil

Pel's Fishing Owl
Visuil

Southern White-faced Owl
Witwanguil

Pearl-spotted Owlet
Witkoluil

African Barred Owlet
Gebande Uil

Western
Barn Owl
Nonnetjie-Uil

Verreaux's
Eagle-Owl
Reuse-Ooruil

Spotted
Eagle-Owl
Gevlekte Ooruil

153

☐ European Nightjar
Europese Naguil

☐ Fiery-necked Nightjar
Afrikaanse Naguil

☐ Freckled Nightjar
Donkernaguil

♂

♀

☐ Pennant-winged Nightjar
Wimpelvlerknaguil

☐ Rufous-cheeked Nightjar
Rooiwangnaguil

☐ Square-tailed Nightjar
Laeveldnaguil

☐ Narina Trogon
Bosloerie

☐ Red-faced Mousebird
Rooiwangmuisvoël

☐ Speckled Mousebird
Gevlekte muisvoël

☐ African Black Swift
Swartwindswael

☐ African Palm Swift
Palmwindswael

☐ Alpine Swift
Witpenswindswael

☐ Common Swift
Europese Windswael

☐ Horus Swift
Horuswindswael

☐ Little Swift
Kleinwindswael

☐ White-rumped Swift
Witkruiswindswael

☐ Böhm's Spinetail
Witpensstekelstert

☐ Mottled Spinetail
Gevlekte Stekelstert

African Pygmy
Kingfisher
Dwergvisvanger

Malachite Kingfisher
Kuifkopvisvanger

Half-collared Kingfisher
Blouvisvanger

Brown-hooded
Kingfisher
Bruinkopvisvanger

Grey-headed Kingfisher
Gryskopvisvanger

Giant Kingfisher
Reusevisvanger

Pied Kingfisher
Bontvisvanger

Striped Kingfisher
Gestreepte visvanger

Woodland Kingfisher
Bosveldvisvanger

Blue-cheeked
Bee-eater
Blouwangbyvreter

European
Bee-eater
Europese Byvreter

Little Bee-eater
Kleinbyvreter

Southern
Carmine Bee-eater
Rooiborsbyvreter

Swallow-tailed
Bee-eater
Swaelstertbyvreter

White-fronted
Bee-eater
Rooikeelbyvreter

157

Broad-billed Roller
Geelbektroupant

European Roller
Europese Troupant

Lilac-breasted Roller
Gewone Troupant

Purple Roller
Groottroupant

Racket-tailed Roller
Knopsterttroupant

Green Wood-Hoopoe
Rooibekkakelaar

African Hoopoe
Hoephoep

Common Scimitarbill
Swartbekkakelaar

African
Grey Hornbill
Grysneushoringvoël

Crowned
Hornbill
Gekroonde Neushoringvoël

Southern
Yellow-billed Hornbill
Geelbekneushoringvoël

Southern
Red-billed Hornbill
Rooibekneushoringvoël

Trumpeter
Hornbill
Gewone Boskraai

Southern
Ground-Hornbill
Bromvoël

♂ ♀ Bearded Woodpecker
Baardspeg

♂ ♀ Bennett's Woodpecker
Bennettspeg

♂ ♀ Cardinal Woodpecker
Kardinaalspeg

♂ ♀ Golden-tailed Woodpecker
Goudstertspeg

♂ ♀ Greater Honeyguide
Grootheuningwyser

Lesser Honeyguide
Kleinheuningwyser

Scaly-throated Honeyguide
Gevlekte Heuningwyser

Brown-backed Honeybird
Skerpbekheuningvoël

☐ Chestnut-backed Sparrowlark
Rooiruglewerik

☐ Dusky Lark
Donkerlewerik

☐ Fawn-coloured Lark
Vaalbruinlewerik

☐ Flappet Lark
Laeveldklappertjie

♂

♀

Grey-backed
☐ Sparrowlark
Grysruglewerik

☐ Monotonous Lark
Bosveldlewerik

☐ Red-capped Lark
Rooikoplewerik

☐ Rufous-naped Lark
Rooineklewerik

☐ Sabota Lark
Sabotalewerik

☐ Bushveld Pipit
Bosveldkoester

Black
Saw-wing
Swartsaagvlerkswael

Brown-throated Martin
Afrikaanse Oewerswael

Common
House-Martin
Huisswael

Rock Martin
Kransswael

Sand Martin
Europese Oewerswael

Barn Swallow
Europese Swael

Grey-rumped Swallow
Gryskruisswael

Lesser
Striped Swallow
Kleinstreepswael

Mosque Swallow
Moskeeswael

Pearl-breasted Swallow
Perelborsswael

Red-breasted
Swallow
Rooiborsswael

White-throated Swallow
Witkeelswael

☐ Wire-tailed Swallow
Draadstertswael

☐ African Pied Wagtail
Bontkwikkie

☐ Cape Wagtail
Gewone Kwikkie

☐ Mountain Wagtail
Bergkwikkie

☐ Western Yellow Wagtail
Geelkwikkie

☐ Yellow-throated Longclaw
Geelkeelkalkoentjie

☐ Plain-backed Pipit
Donkerkoester

☐ Striped Pipit
Gestreepte Koester

☐ African Pipit
Gewone Koester

☐ Buffy Pipit
Vaalkoester

☐ Black Cuckooshrike
Swartkatakoeroe

☐ White-breasted Cuckooshrike
Witborskatakoeroe

163

Terrestrial Brownbul
Boskrapper

Dark-capped Bulbul
Swartoogtiptol

Sombre Greenbul
Gewone Willie

Yellow-bellied Greenbul
Geelborswillie

Willow Warbler
Hofsanger

Stierling's Wren-Warbler
Stierlingsanger

Burnt-necked Eremomela
Buinkeelbossanger

Green-capped Eremomela
Donkerwangbossanger

Yellow-bellied Eremomela
Geelpensbossanger

Bar-throated Apalis
Bandkeel-kleinjantjie

Rudd's Apalis
Ruddkleinjantjie

Yellow-breasted Apalis
Geelborskleinjantjie

Croaking Cisticola
Groot Tinktinkie

Desert Cisticola
Woestynklopkloppie

Lazy Cisticola
Luitinktinkie

Rattling Cisticola
Bosveldtinktinkie

Red-faced Cisticola
Rooiwangtinktinkie

Rufous-winged Cisticola
Swartrugtinktinkie

Zitting Cisticola
Landeryklopkloppie

Green-backed
Camaroptera
Groenrugkwekwevoël

Grey-backed
Camaroptera
Grysrugkwekwevoël

Neddicky
Neddikie

Tawny-flanked Prinia
Bruinsylangstertjie

Long-billed Crombec
Bosveldstompstert

☐ African Reed Warbler
Kleinrietsanger

☐ Broad-tailed Warbler
Breëstertsanger

☐ Dark-capped Yellow Warbler
Geelsanger

☐ Garden Warbler
Tuinsanger

☐ Great Reed Warbler
Grootrietsanger

☐ Icterine Warbler
Spotsanger

☐ Lesser Swamp Warbler
Kaapse Rietsanger

☐ Little Rush Warbler
Kaapse vleisanger

☐ Marsh Warbler
Europese Rietsanger

☐ Olive-tree Warbler
Olyfboomsanger

☐ River Warbler
Sprinkaansanger

☐ Sedge Warbler
Europese Vleisanger

☐ Southern Hyliota
Mashonahyliota

☐ Common Whitethroat
Witkeelsanger

Chestnut-vented
☐ Tit-Babbler
Bosveldtjeriktik

☐ Collared Palm-Thrush
Palmmorelyster

☐ Groundscraper Thrush
Gevlekte Lyster

☐ Kurrichane Thrush
Rooibeklyster

☐ Capped Wheatear
Hoëveldskaapwagter

☐ African Stonechat
Gewone Bontrokkie

☐ Cape Robin-Chat
Gewone Janfrederik

☐ Red-capped
Robin-Chat
Nataljanfrederik

☐ White-browed
Robin-Chat
Heuglinjanfrederik

☐ White-throated
Robin-Chat
Witkeeljanfrederik

Bearded Scrub Robin
Baardwipstert

White-browed
Scrub Robin
Gestreepte Wipstert

Thrush Nightingale
Lysternagtegaal

Arnot's Chat
Bontpiek

Familiar Chat
Gewone Spekvreter

Mocking Cliff Chat
Dassievoël

Ashy Flycatcher
Blougrysvlieevanger

African
Dusky Flycatcher
Donkervlieevanger

Fiscal Flycatcher
Fiskaalvlieevanger

Grey Tit-Flycatcher
Waaierstertvlieevanger

Marico Flycatcher
Maricovlieevanger

Pale Flycatcher
Muiskleurvlieevanger

Southern Black Flycatcher
Swartvlieevanger

Spotted Flycatcher
Europese Vlieevanger

Cape Batis
Kaapse Bosbontrokkie

Chinspot Batis
Witliesbosbontrokkie

Black-throated Wattle-eye
Beloogbosbontrokkie

African Paradise Flycatcher
Paradysvlieevanger

Blue-mantled Crested-Flycatcher
Bloukuifvlieevanger

Arrow-marked Babbler
Pylvlekkatlagter

Crested Barbet
Kuifkophoutkapper

Acacia Pied Barbet
Bonthoutkapper

Black-collared Barbet
Rooihoutkapper

Yellow-fronted Tinkerbird
Geelblestinker

169

Yellow-rumped Tinkerbird
Swartblestinker

Amethyst Sunbird
Swartsuikerbekkie

Collared Sunbird
Kortbeksuikerbekkie

Marico Sunbird
Maricosuikerbekkie

Purple-banded Sunbird
Purperbandsuikerbekkie

Scarlet-chested Sunbird
Rooiborssuikerbekkie

White-bellied Sunbird
Witpenssuikerbekkie

African Yellow White-eye
Geelglasogie

Cape White-eye
Kaapse Glasogie

Southern Black Tit
Gewone Swartmees

Grey Penduline Tit
Gryskapokvoël

Eastern Nicator
Geelvleknikator

African Golden Oriole
Afrikaanse Wielewaal

Black-headed Oriole
Swartkopwielewaal

Eurasian Golden Oriole
Europese Wielewaal

Crimson-breasted Shrike
Rooiborslaksman

Lesser Grey Shrike
Gryslaksman

Magpie Shrike
Langstertlaksman

♂ ♀

Red-backed Shrike
Rooiruglaksman

Southern White-crowned Shrike
Kremetartlaksman

Southern (Common) Fiscal
Fiskaallaksman

Fork-tailed Drongo
Mikstertbyvanger

171

♂
♀

Southern Boubou
Suidelike Waterfiskaal

Tropical Boubou
Tropiese Waterfiskaal

Brubru
Bontroklaksman

Gorgeous Bush-Shrike
Konkoit

Grey-headed
Bush-Shrike
Spookvoël

Olive
Bush-Shrike
Olyfboslaksman

Orange-breasted Bush-
Shrike
Oranjeborsboslaksman

Black-backed
Puffback
Sneeubal

Black-crowned Tchagra
Swaartkroontjagra

Brown-crowned
Tchagra
Rooivlerktjagra

Retz's
Helmet-Shrike
Swarthelmlaksman

White-crested
Helmet-Shrike
Withelmlaksman

Red-billed Oxpecker
Rooibekrenostervoël

Yellow-billed Oxpecker
Geelbekrenostervoël

Common Myna
Indiese Spreeu

Pied Crow
Witborskraai

Black-bellied Starling
Swartpensglansspreeu

Burchell's Starling
Grootglansspreeu

Cape Glossy Starling
Kleinglansspreeu

Greater Blue-eared Starling
Grootblouoorglansspreeu

Meves's Starling
Langstertglansspreeu

Red-winged Starling
Rooivlerkspreeu

Violet-backed Starling
Witborsspreeu

Wattled Starling
Lelspreeu

173

White-browed Sparrow-Weaver
Koringvoël

African (Holub's) Golden Weaver
Goudwewer

Lesser Masked-Weaver
Kleingeelvink

Red-billed Buffalo Weaver
Buffelwewer

Red-headed Weaver
Rooikopwewer

Southern Brown-throated Weaver
Bruinkeelwewer

Southern Masked Weaver
Swartkeelgeelvink

Spectacled Weaver
Brilwewer

Thick-billed Weaver
Dikbekwewer

Village Weaver
Bontrugwewer

Yellow Weaver
Kaapse wewer / Geelwewer

174

Fan-tailed Widowbird
Kortstertflap

Red-collared Widowbird
Rooikeelflap

White-winged Widowbird
Witvlerkflap

Red-billed Quelea
Rooibekkwelea

Southern Red Bishop
Rooivink

Yellow-crowned Bishop
Goudgeelvink

Cuckoo Finch
Koekoekvink

Cut-throat Finch
Bandkeelvink

Red-headed Finch
Rooikopvink

African Firefinch
Kaapse Vuurvinkie

Jameson's Firefinch
Jamesonvuurvinkie

Red-billed Firefinch
Rooibekvuurvinkie

☐ Green-winged Pytilia
Gewone Melba

☐ Orange-winged Pytilia
Oranjevlerkmelba

☐ African Quail-finch
Gewone Kwartelvinkie

☐ Bronze Mannikin
Gewone Fret

☐ Red-backed Mannikin
Rooirugfret

☐ Green Twinspot
Groenkolpensie

☐ Pink-throated Twinspot
Rooskeelkolpensie

☐ Blue Waxbill
Gewone Blousysie

☐ Common Waxbill
Rooibeksysie

☐ Orange-breasted Waxbill
Rooiassie

☐ Violet-eared Waxbill
Koningblousysie

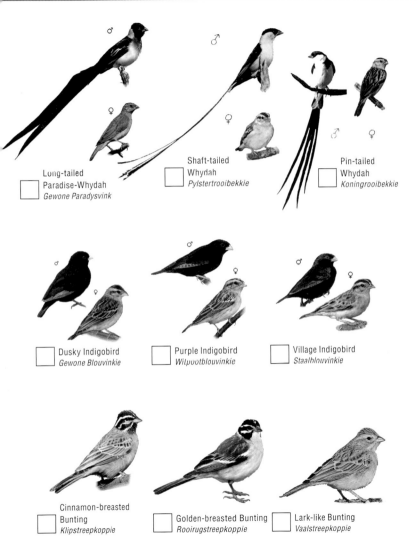

Long-tailed
Paradise-Whydah
Gewone Paradysvink

Shaft-tailed
Whydah
Pylstertrooibekkie

Pin-tailed
Whydah
Koningrooibekkie

Dusky Indigobird
Gewone Blouvinkie

Purple Indigobird
Witpootblouvinkie

Village Indigobird
Staalblouvinkie

Cinnamon-breasted
Bunting
Klipstreepkoppie

Golden-breasted Bunting
Rooirugstreepkoppie

Lark-like Bunting
Vaalstreepkoppie

Brimstone Canary
Dikbekkanarie

Lemon-breasted Canary
Geelborskanarie

Yellow-fronted Canary
Geeloogkanarie

Streaky-headed Seedeater
Streepkopkanarie

Yellow-throated Petronia
Geelvlekmossie

Cape Sparrow
Gewone mossie

House Sparrow
Huismossie

Southern Grey-headed Sparrow
Gryskopmossie

Southern Ground-Hornbill

Tracks

Animals are not always where one wants them to be, but at least they leave tracks for us to follow. Tracking spoor can be a lot of fun. The following double page illustrates the most common tracks you may encounter. Footprints left by large predators and some of the big herbivores can give a good indication of what may be lurking in the bush.

Front
13–14.5cm

Hind
12–15cm

Lion

Front
8–10cm

Hind
9–10cm

Leopard

Front
±30cm

Hind
±30cm

White Rhino

Front
±24cm

Hind
±23cm

Black Rhino

Front
±50cm

Hind
±50cm

Elephant

Front
±12cm

Hind
±12cm

Buffalo